Lea
the Solar System

Bruce LaFontaine

DOVER PUBLICATIONS, INC.
Mineola, New York

Bibliographical Note

Learning About the Solar System is a new work, first published by
Dover Publications, Inc., in 2000.

International Standard Book Number: 0-486-41009-9

Manufactured in the United States of America
Dover Publications, Inc., 31 East 2nd Street, Mineola, N.Y. 11501

Introduction

Nine planets—Mercury, Venus, Earth, Mars, Jupiter, Saturn, Uranus, Neptune, and Pluto—orbit the Sun, the fiery star at the center of our solar system. Both Saturn and Uranus have ring systems, and many of the planets have moons, satellites orbiting them. Comets, huge balls of ice and rocks, orbit the Sun as well. As you read about the solar system in this little book, you'll learn interesting facts about each of the planets and also be able to illustrate each page with a colorful sticker.

The Sun

diameter: approx. 870,000 miles

The Sun is a fiery star at the center of our solar system. Nine planets, including the Earth, orbit the Sun, along with comets and asteroids. A ball of hydrogen gas, the Sun has a surface temperature of 10,000°F; its core averages 27,000,000°F. Its dark "sun spots" are relatively cooler— about 6,000°F.

Mercury

diameter: 3,032 miles
distance from Sun: 43 million miles

Mercury, the planet closest to the Sun, is covered with craters and cracks. The second smallest planet in our solar system, Mercury takes only 88 Earth days to orbit the Sun. The side of Mercury that faces the Sun has a blistering temperature of 620°F; the far side reaches a chilling 346°F below zero.

Venus

diameter: 7,521 miles
distance from Sun: 67 million miles

Venus, second planet from the Sun, is often called the "evening star"—it is the first and brightest object seen in the night sky. Venus has a thick, cloudy atmosphere of deadly carbon dioxide and sulfuric acid. The temperature on its rocky surface reaches 850°F. No Earth-type life forms could survive there.

Earth

diameter: 7,927 miles
distance from Sun: 93 million miles

Earth is the only planet in the solar
system known to have life forms. As
third planet from the Sun, Earth is at
a proper distance to have liquid
water, needed to support life.
Seventy percent of Earth is covered
by oceans and seas. The rest is land
mass (the seven continents).

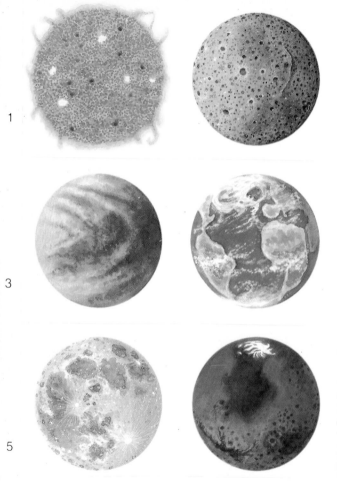

1

3

5

AFTER ALL THE STICKERS HAVE BEEN PLACED IN THE CORRECT SPACES
PLEASE GENTLY REMOVE AND DISCARD THESE TWO PAGES

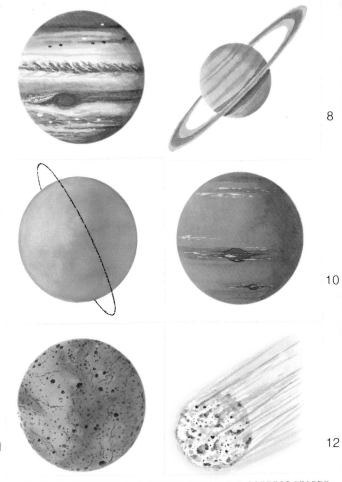

8

10

12

AFTER ALL THE STICKERS HAVE BEEN PLACED IN THE CORRECT SPACES
PLEASE GENTLY REMOVE AND DISCARD THESE TWO PAGES   41009-9

The Moon

diameter: 2,159 miles
distance from Earth: approx. 252,000 miles

Earth has a large natural satellite, the Moon (Luna). Its terrain is covered with craters, cracks, and large, smooth basins. Scientists believe that it was formed when the Earth was struck long ago by a huge object; the resulting fragments bonded together over billions of years to form the Moon.

5

Mars

diameter: 4,212 miles
distance from Sun: 141 million miles

Mars, the fourth planet, is a cold, dry, desert world. It is possible that, long ago, Mars was once warmer and had liquid water on its surface, allowing for primitive life. A fossilized bacteria, possibly from this earlier period, was discovered recently. Exploring Mars is the goal of many space missions.

[Sticker #7]

Jupiter

diameter: 88,000 miles
distance from Sun: 483 million miles

Jupiter is the fifth planet from the
Sun and the largest in our solar system. It is one of four planets known
as "Gas Giants," planets composed
almost entirely of gases. One of its
moons, Europa, might possibly have
life forms in an ocean believed to be
under its icy crust.

Saturn

diameter: 74,000 miles
distance from Sun: 886 million miles

The sixth planet from the Sun is
Saturn. Its colorful ring system is
made up of ice, rocks, and dust.
Second largest of the "Gas Giants,"
Saturn has the most known moons
(23) of any planet. Some scientists
believe that the moon Titan may
have rivers, lakes, and even oceans
of liquid methane.

Uranus

diameter: 32,000 miles
distance from Sun: 1 billion 700 million miles

Seventh planet from the Sun, the "Gas Giant" Uranus has a blue-green surface with no visible features. Uranus spins on its axis at an almost vertical angle; the other planets spin horizontally. Uranus also has a ring system like Saturn's, but much smaller. The planet is orbited by fifteen moons.

Neptune

diameter: 30,800 miles
distance from Sun: 2 billion 790 million miles

The eighth planet from the Sun and smallest of the "Gas Giants" is distant Neptune. Space probes sent from Earth have recorded the coldest temperature ever found on any planetary body on Neptune's icy moon Triton. Neptune has a huge cyclone-like storm on its surface whose diameter is larger than Earth's.

Pluto

diameter: 1,860 miles
distance from Sun: 3 billion 780 million miles

Pluto is the ninth and last planet in our solar system. It is so distant, it is the only planet not photographed by Earth-launched robotic space probes. It is named an "icy dwarf" because of its comparatively small size and ice-covered surface. The diameter of Charon, its moon, is one third that of Pluto's.

Comets

Size and distance from Sun vary greatly.

Comets are huge balls of ice, rocks, and dust that orbit the Sun at very great distances. A comet has a "head" and a "tail." The head may range from ten miles in diameter to 1,000 miles. The tail, a trail of vaporizing gases, is what we see from Earth.